Perishable Poems

Poèmes Périssables

DIÁLOGOS
BOOKS
dialogosbooks.com

Acknowledgements

The translator is indebted to Roger Williams University for the sabbatical leave that made this work possible. Hats, and fezzes, off to *Narrative Magazine* for making one of these poems ("Reader In A Rush") "Poem of The Week." A heartfelt thank you to Abdellatif Laâbi for kind permission to reprint. Though these are poems of aftermath, they are the aftermath of the kind of political struggle that Diálogos Books has generously adopted as its mission, and which continues every day.

Foreword

Here we are, finally, at the moment when Abdellatif
Laâbi needs no introduction to Anglophone readers. This is
thanks to recent translations hosted by Carcanet, City Lights,
Archipelago and others. We now join Africans and Africa
scholars in recognizing him as Morocco's preeminent living
poet, winner of France's Prix Goncourt and Grand Prix de La
Francophonie, a poet who shares a well-lighted stage with the
best-selling novelist Tahar Ben Jelloun. This recognition has
been an uncertain journey—first interrupted by imprisonment,
then accelerated by great productivity in the years that Laâbi
has lived in France. *Perishable Poems* is a substantial volume
and, like most in recent years (including a volume of collected
works), was brought out by Editions de La Différence (2000,
Collection Clepsydre).

The recent prestige of this poetry might still obscure,
for English readers, the variety of Laâbi's other work. His
autobiography is *Le Fond la Jarre*, 2004 (*The Bottom of The Jar*).
One of the first books to be translated adds to the autobiography:
Rue du Retour. (The book has this French title, though it is in
English; the French title is *Le Chemin des Ordalies*, 1982.) He
writes novels and plays. And he is an important translator—
sometimes in collaboration with his wife Jocelyne—from
Arabic. Notably, he has translated Mahmoud Darwish.

Laâbi's fame, and his troubles, grew in the 1960s. When
he founded the journal *Souffles* it was, at first, a venue for
Morocco's writers and not a forum for the politics that would

attract the government's ire. When this journal, and the journal *Anfas*, became more political Laâbi was arrested (1972). There are allusions to his imprisonment and torture in several works, including *Perishable Poems*:

I live
with fear in my gut
Fear of what?
Of the apocalypse announced
and boringly commented
Of love's drying up
and writing too
Of the torturer I thought I'd forgotten
who has not forgotten me
Of doing something ignominious
Of catching the disease of submission
Or of dying randomly
run over like a dog?

Rue du Retour also tells much of this story, and describes the adjustment to life after jail. Laâbi's sentence was commuted in 1980, and he was finally able to exile himself in France in the mid-1980s.

The present volume is a quiet one, less suggestive and startling than receptive. Not receptive like a surrealist's receptivity to the results of experiment—but receptive like a fifty-eight year old man's reevaluation of life. These poems gently question the yield of disparate episodes in a long life—and of experiences more harrowing than most of us can understand. They ask "What page will collect your cries/and the dry ink of our tears?" They assert uncertainty: "I didn't hear/my sentence handed down." And a vague alienation: "They seem in every way like men/and they are not men." They are specific about a few things: age, prison, love. One element in particular is poignant and evocative of much North African writing, while also proper to the present passage of Laâbi's life: exile. "The red roof tiles/sharpen the illusion/I am not/where I think I am." "Outside/the town doesn't know I'm here." These lines situate the poet near Paris, extend his exile indefinitely, and transcribe the quotidian observations and quiet questions to a minor key, a sustained note of what is missing.

It would be a mistake to think this book is thus made hollow, a work that suffers from a lack. The book is shaped around what is missing, and what is eternally questioned, and the final result is elegant. Consider that this is a fairly lengthy volume, with powerful poems of greater length at the beginning and end. The very brief poems in the middle perhaps underline Laâbi's sense of the "perishable." There is some irony in his use of the word; he came close to perishing in prison. The brevity of some poems gains enormous weight, and the poems gain emotional thrust, through every North African's awareness of Laâbi's persecution. No one reads poems such as "I pretend to live" without thinking of his imprisonment and torture. Laâbi perhaps suggests that, like his physical self, these poems are lasting, or not—essential, or not. "My hand stayed open/till I no longer felt it." If anything is lasting, in many of these *natures mortes*, it is some kind of question.

So *Perishable Poems* is a text within a text—the latter being the story of imprisonment. Safoi Babana-Hampton notes this "spectral return" of prison days in an article about several Laâbi works ("Le retour spectral du passé carcéral dans les écrits de prison d'Abdellatif Laâbi"). All of this now plays within yet another text, that of Arab Spring and authoritarian abuses. It has been thirty-six years since Laâbi's prose account of his release from prison. The passions and disappointments of Arab Spring (which Morocco's king largely side-stepped and on which Moroccan poet Mohamed Loakira comments in *...and spring is veiled over*, 2018 [*...et se voile le printemps*, 2015]) shine a light both human and harsh on authoritarianism—and on the life that flowers again after the cruelest repression.

—Peter Thompson

Abdellatif Laâbi

Perishable Poems

Poèmes Périssables

Translated by
Peter Thompson

DIÁLOGOS
BOOKS
New Orleans

Poèmes Périssables

Perishable Poems

I

I

Le lecteur pressé

Que viens-tu faire ici
lecteur ?
Tu as ouvert sans ménagement
ce livre
et tu remues fébrilement le sable des pages
à la recherche
de je ne sais quel trésor enfoui
Es-tu là pour pleurer
ou pour rire
N'as-tu personne d'autre
à qui parler
Ta vie
est-elle à ce point vide ?
Alors referme vite ce livre
Pose-le loin du réveille-matin
et de la boîte à médicaments
Laisse-le mûrir
au soleil du désir
sur la branche du beau silence

Reader in a Rush

What did you come here to do
reader?
With nothing in mind you opened
this book
and feverishly you shift the sand of its pages
seeking I know not
what buried treasure
Are you here to cry then
or to laugh
Have you no one else
to talk to
Your life
is really that empty?
Then close the book quickly
Put it far from the alarm clock
and the bottle of pills
Let it ripen
in the rays of desire
on the branch of gorgeous silence

Je n'ai pas changé

Je n'ai pas changé
depuis la dernière fois

Si la pénombre
pouvait douter d'elle-même
Si je pouvais dénouer
une seule énigme
de l'océan de mes ignorances
Si ma vie
m'était contée comme une histoire
dont on devinerait
la fin heureuse

Non
je n'ai pas changé
J'ai simplement moins de temps
que la dernière fois

I Haven't Changed

I haven't changed
since last time

If the gloaming
could doubt itself
If I could unravel
a single riddle
in the ocean of my ignorances
If my life
were told me like a story
where you might guess
the happy ending

No
I haven't changed
I just have less time
than last time

Inséparables

Pauvre corps
étriqué et mal foutu
Je te remercie de ton hospitalité

Tu pousses la tolérance
jusqu'au vice

J'en profite sans vergogne

Je t'use
et tu m'uses

Inséparables nous sommes
mais pas dupes

Inseparable

Poor body
scrawny and played out too
I thank you for your hospitality

You are tolerant
to a fault

Shamelessly I take advantage

I use you up
as you do me

Inseparable we may be
but never duped

Demain sera le même jour

Demain
sera le même jour
Je n'aurai vécu que quelques instants
le front collé à la vitre
pour accueillir le carrousel du crépuscule
J'aurai étouffé un cri
car personne ne l'aura entendu
en ce désert
Je me serai mis
dans la position du fœtus
sur le siège de ma vieille solitude
J'aurai attendu
que mon verre se vide à moitié
pour y déceler le goût du fiel
Je me serai vu
le lendemain
me réveillant et vaquant
Atrocement semblable

Tomorrow Will Be the Same Day

Tomorrow
will be the same day
I will have lived only moments
my forehead stuck to the pane
to greet the carousel of dusk
I will have stifled a cry
because no one could have heard it
in this wilderness
I will have gotten myself
into fetal position
on the bench of my age-old solitude
I will have waited
for my glass to be half empty
to pick up then the taste of spleen
I will have seen myself
the next day
waking and stumbling vacant
Atrociously the same

Des rêves à la pelle

Des rêves à la pelle
comme si mes jours débordaient
et que ma plume était verte
Je dors avec mes ombres
et me réveille sans
O nuit
résiste
Le dieu de l'aube
dévore tes enfants

Dreams by the Bucketful

Dreams by the bucket
as if my days were overflowing
and my pen were green
I sleep with my shadows
and awake with none
Oh night
hold fast
The god of dawn
devours your children

Les images périmées

Maintenant j'écris
comme l'aveugle voit
La lumière glisse sur mes paupières
et s'évacue par le trou de la page
Les mots font les cent pas dans leur cage
J'entends claquer le fouet du dompteur
et pas de rugissement
Mes images toutes
sont périmées
Je marche
dans le dédale du cœur
sans chien-guide

Outdated Images

Now I write
the way the blind man sees
Light glides over my lids
and drains through the hole of the page
Words pace endlessly in their cage
I hear the tamer's whip
but no roaring
My images are all
outdated
I walk
in the heart's maze
with no guide dog

Je rappelle la nuit à ses devoirs

Je rappelle la nuit à ses devoirs :
offre-moi du sommeil
la fourrure imprévue du désir
Un arbre qui m'épouse
et me protège de la furie de l'errance
Une présence même furtive
de mes chers disparus
Un regain de visions
qui ne s'apparentent pas au cauchemar
Des mots qui parfument la bouche
et font jaillir la source sous ma langue
Offre-moi
en guise d'aube
une montée de lait
au goût d'innocence
Eloigne de moi le coq maudit
Viens sur moi
Appose tes bracelets
sur mes mamelons endurcis
Fais sortir de mon flanc
l'oiseau bleu
Prends mon vertige
et rends-le moi
Laisse-moi dans l'ignorance
de ta défaite imminente
Ne pars pas
Ne me jette pas en pâture
à la trompeuse lumière du jour

I Remind the Night of Its Duties

I remind the night of its duties:
offer me some sleep
the unexpected furs of desire
A tree to marry me
and protect me from the rage of straying
A presence however furtive
of my loved ones gone
A revival of visions
unlinked to nightmare
Words that scent the mouth
and make a spring leap under my tongue
Offer me
as a kind of dawn
a surging of milk
 tasting like innocence
Drive the rooster of evil away
Come onto me
Put your metal rings
against my hardened nipples
Make the blue bird flap
out of my side
Take my dizziness
and then give it back
Leave me unaware
of your imminent defeat
Don't leave
Don't put me to pasture
in the deceiving light of day

Tard dans la vie

Tard dans la vie
je pourrai m'absenter sur un banc
la douleur en moins
J'éteindrai le feu
des passions qui ont écourté le voyage
J'arrêterai la litanie
des questions vieillies avec les réponses
Je sortirai du champ
de la vision incohérente
Je tatouerai sur ma paume
mon dernier petit poème d'amour
et je m'endormirai
du sommeil délicieux
de l'arbre

Late in Life

Late in life
I'll be able to just drift on a bench
pain growing less
I'll damp the flame
of the passions that have shortened the trip
I'll stop the litany
of questions grown old and their answers
I'll step out of the field
of incoherent vision
I'll tattoo on my palm
my last little love poem
and I'll fall asleep
with the delicious slumber
of a tree

Le poète anonyme

Est-ce ma voix
ou celle d'un poète anonyme
venant des siècles obscurs
Quand ai-je vécu
Sur quelle terre
Quelle femme ai-je aimée
De quelle passion
Et puis qui me dit
que je n'étais pas justement une femme
et que je n'ai pas connu d'homme
parce que trop laide
ou n'ayant simplement pas d'attirance
pour les hommes
Me suis-je battu
pour
contre quelque chose
Ai-je eu la foi
des enfants
Suis-je mort jeune
incompris, misérable
ou très vieux, entouré, adulé
héraut d'une tribu se préparant
à conquérir le monde
Mes œuvres m'ont-elles survécu
Ma langue est-elle morte
avant que d'être écrite
Mais d'abord étais-je aède
ou roi fainéant
prêtre
pleureuse professionnelle

The Anonymous Poet

Is this my voice
or that of an anonymous poet
arriving from the murk of centuries
When did I live
On what earth
What woman did I love
With what passion
Then again who says
I wasn't in fact a woman
one who never had a man
being too ugly
or simply not attracted
to men
Did I fight
for
against anything
Had I the faith
a child has
Did I die young
misunderstood miserable
or very old, surrounded, worshipped
herald of a tribe preparing
to conquer the world
Did my works survive
Did my language die
before it was written
But first was I homeric chanter
or layabout king
priest
professional mourner

navigateur
djinn ou adamite
savante almée
jouant du luth dans un harem ?
Peut-être n'étais-je
qu'un artisan sellier
n'ayant jamais monté à cheval
et qui chantait
en trimant la sainte journée
pour que le cuir se ramollisse entre ses mains
et rende de la belle ouvrage
qu'enfourcheront les riches

Alors qui étais-je
pour que ma parole se dédouble
et que le malin sosie
qui en tient les rênes
me piège
avec cette question qui n'en est pas une :
est-ce ta voix
ou celle d'un poète anonyme
venant des siècles obscurs ?

navigator
genie or adamite
Egyptian dancer
playing my lute in a harem?
Perhaps I was only
an artisan saddler
never having ridden a horse
a saddler singing
and toiling through the holy day
to make the leather soften in his hands
and yield a fine tooling
to be straddled by the rich

Who was I then
that my speech was split in two
and the malignant double
who holds its reins
traps me
with this question that isn't:
is it your voice
or an anonymous poet's
arriving from the murk of ages?

Je scrute le ciel

Je scrute le ciel à l'œil nu
et tends l'oreille
O vous
des galaxies en fuite
au-delà du trou noir
répondez-moi
Un mot de vous
et je m'inscrirai
à la prochaine aventure
J'enterrerai ma peur
dans le lourd suaire
de mes manques

I Scrutinize the Sky

I scrutinize the sky, eyes peeled
and tilt my ear
Oh you
of the galaxies retreating
beyond the black hole
answer me
One word from you
and I'll sign up
for the next adventure
I will bury my fear
in the heavy shroud
of my failings

Le carré des étrangers

Quoi qu'il arrive
je reposerai en la terre
qui m'aura donné asile
Où que ce soit
mon ultime demeure
sera
au carré des étrangers

The Foreigners' Square

Whatever happens
I will rest in whatever land
has given me asylum
Wherever this be
my final resting place
will be
the foreigners' patch

II

II

Trois petits arbres
trop jeunes
pour me donner la réplique

C'est moi
le merle empesé
qui vient de passer
en silence

Comme lui
je suis habillé de noir

Je vole assis

Les barreaux du ciel
sont solides

Je ne peux chanter
de si bon matin

Three little trees
too young
to cue my lines

It's me
the stiff blackbird
who's just passed
silently by

Like him
I am dressed in black

I fly seated like this

The bars of the sky
are solid

I cannot sing
this early

Le frisson
qui précède le mot
d'où viendra-t-il ?
Il y a ces eaux du Détroit
charriant les oiseaux chassés d'Afrique
Cette chambre d'hôtel
où la fenêtre indiscrète
s'oppose au désir
Ce diadème de cimetières
posé sur la poitrine
de la ville endormie
Il y a ce mur à franchir
bête à en pleurer
Ce ciel court
l'étau de ses nuages

En somme rien
qu'on puisse mettre
au compte de la vie

The shiver
just before the word
where does it come from?
There are those waters in the Straits
bearing birds chased out of Africa
This hotel room
where an indiscreet window
is opposed to desire
This diadem of cemeteries
resting on the chest
of the sleeping town
There is this wall to cross
dumb as the day is long
This sky darts
through the vise of its clouds

In all nothing
you would charge
against life's account

Ma fenêtre
avare et stupide
Autant ouvrir la porte
qui donne sur le couloir

My window
greedy and dumb
Might as well open the door
onto the hallway

Allez donc écrire un poème
sur une voiture
O mes ancêtres chameliers
si vous saviez !

So go write a poem
about a car
Oh my camel-driving forebears
if you only knew!

Pour la moindre miette de liberté
je dois encore galérer
Pour la plus petite vérité
je dois encore me faire violence
O mère
quelle esclave étais-tu
lorsque tu m'as conçu ?

For the slightest crumb of freedom
I still must pine in the galleys
For the tiniest truth
I still must lash myself
Oh mother
what slave were you
the day you conceived me?

Ceci est ma maison
éphémère comme les précédentes
Les objets sont à la place
que je leur ai désignée
Demain
je déménagerai
et ils me suivront
D'eux ou de moi
qui est le plus exilé ?

This is my house
ephemeral as the ones before it
The objects are in the places
I have designated
Tomorrow
I will move out
and they will follow me
Between them and me
who is more exiled?

Ecrire
pour différer la mort
précipiter la vie
L'angoisse est la même

Mon âme
m'appartient
Pourquoi devrais-je la rendre ?

Writing
to put off death
or hurry life
The anguish is the same

My soul
belongs to me
Why should I yield it up?

Plutôt que sens
donner consistance
à la vie

Rituels
sans magie
Routine de l'être

Rather than meaning
give consistency
to life

Rituals
minus the magic
Being's routine

Je recueille bout par bout
ce qui subsiste en moi
Tessons de colère
lambeaux de passion
escarbilles de joie
Je couds, colle et cautérise
Abracadabra !
Je suis de nouveau debout
Pour quelle autre bataille ?

I gather up scrap by scrap
all that is left in me
Shards of anger
shreds of passion
cinders of joy
I sew, glue and cauterize
Abracadabra!
On my feet once again
For what new battle?

Quand le quotidien m'use
je m'abuse
en y mettant mon grain d'ironie
Voici le chat
et voici la souris
Auteur méconnu de dessins animés
je suis

When the quotidian wears me down
I give myself illusions
while adding my speck of irony
Here is the cat
and here the mouse
Unrecognized author of cartoons
am I

Incrustés dans le mur
des yeux s'ouvrent
d'autres se referment
A la question incongrue
l'absence de lèvres
est une réponse cinglante

Inlaid in the wall
eyes open
and others close
To the inappropriate question
the absence of any lips
is a bullwhip response

Quand on n'a plus à offrir
que le mal de vivre
le ridicule de la douleur
autant se taire

Quelle indécence déjà à se le dire
en croyant toucher
à je ne sais quel art !

When you have nothing more to offer
than the ills of living
the absurdity of pain
you might as well be quiet

What indecency, going on about it
while thinking it rises
to some kind of art!

J'ai cru par l'esprit
me libérer de mes prisons
Mais l'esprit lui-même
est une prison
J'ai essayé d'en repousser les parois
J'essaie toujours

I thought that through my mind
I'd get free of my prisons
But the mind itself
is a prison
I've tried to push out the walls
I'm still trying

Le corps
un réduit
Le supplicié compte les jours
De ce réduit
on ne s'échappe pas
Les coups
sont portés de l'intérieur
L'aveu ne sert à rien
Quel aveu d'ailleurs ?
S'accuser d'être homme ?

The body
a hovel
The tortured count their days
From this hovel
you don't escape
The blows
are swung from within
Confession does no good
And what confession anyway?
Admitting you are human?

C'est ma nuit
pas la vôtre
Elle me présente son calice
et je bois
me soulage
du fardeau de ma tête
Je vais oublier
sans fermer les yeux
Rien ne m'arrivera
ni heur ni malheur
Je vais entrer dans une autre attente
et l'attente
je m'y connais
bien avant ma naissance

This is my night
not yours
It brings me its chalice
and I drink
soothe myself
of the burden of my head
I will forget
but not close my eyes
Nothing will happen to me
not happiness nor unhappiness
I'll step into another waiting
and waiting
is something I know about
since way before birth

L'énigme s'est rhabillée
après la longue étreinte
Je me lève
et quitte
le tombeau de ma souveraine

Enigma has gotten dressed again
after our long embrace
I rise
and leave
the tomb of my queen

Parfois je vis
Parfois je meurs
Plus près de la blessure
Plus loin des mots

Sometimes I live
Sometimes I die
Closer to the wound
Farther from words

Le pilleur des rêves
est encore passé
Au rêveur
il n'a laissé
qu'un goût de sable
dans la bouche

The plunderer of dreams
has come by again
For the dreamer
he has left only
a taste of sand
in the mouth

Laver son cœur
le faire sécher
le repasser
le suspendre sur un cintre
Ne pas le replacer tout de suite
dans sa cage
Attendre
la clé charnelle de la vision
l'impossible retour
le dénouement de l'éternité

To wash your heart
dry it out
iron it
drape it on a coat hanger
And not put it back right away
in its cage
To await
the carnal key to vision
the impossible return
the denouement of eternity

Quelle lune de sa lame lacère le poème ?
Amours défuntes, amours en gésine
quelle page recueillera vos cris
et l'encre sèche de nos larmes ?

What moon slashes the poem with its blade?
Loves now dead, loves laid out
what page will collect your cries
and the dry ink of our tears?

Je vis
la peur au ventre
Peur de quoi ?
De l'apocalypse annoncée
et péniblement reportée
Du tarissement de l'amour
de l'écriture
Du bourreau que j'ai cru oublier
et qui ne m'a pas encore oublié
De commettre quelque ignominie
D'attraper la maladie de la soumission
Ou de mourir par hasard
écrasé comme un chien ?

I live
with fear in my gut
Fear of what?
Of the apocalypse announced
and boringly commented
Of love's drying up
and writing too
Of the torturer I thought I'd forgotten
who has not forgotten me
Of doing something ignominious
Of catching the disease of submission
Or of dying randomly
run over like a dog?

III

III

Si tu veux
ne pas être trop déçu
prépare-toi
à la déception

If you want
to not be too disappointed
get ready
for disappointment

Je fais semblant de vivre
L'effort est louable
puisqu'il faut absolument
payer de retour
cette chienne de vie

I pretend to live
The effort is laudable
since you absolutely must
pay back
this bitch of a life

La tristesse
n'est pas mon métier
Mais comme elle est rare
la joie pure !

Sadness
is not my stock in trade
But look how rare
is pure joy!

Le gouffre
que je scrute depuis si longtemps
ce n'est que le vide
que je refuse de voir en moi

The abyss
I've pondered for so long
it is only the emptiness
I refuse to see in me

Je ris
et fais rire
pour surmonter l'indécence

Il en faut de l'inconscience
pour ressentir du bonheur

Ma main est restée ouverte
jusqu'à ce que je ne la sente plus

I laugh
and make others laugh
to overcome indecency

Unconsciousness is what you need
to feel happiness

My hand stayed open
till I no longer felt it

Où est l'amour
qui devine en toi la noire tempête
et l'arrête
d'un simple souffle d'entre ses lèvres ?

Où est l'ami
qui t'appelle
juste pour te dire bonjour ?

Où est le pays
qui ne te réclame pas
chaque année
le prix de ta naissance ?

Where is the love
that divines the black storm in you
and halts it with just a puff from her lips?

Where is the friend
who calls you
just to say hello?

Where is the country
that doesn't demand from you
yearly
the price of your birth?

Un mot m'échappe
et c'est comme si je ne savais plus parler
Il faut que je le retrouve
sinon
je suis un homme mort
à mes yeux

A word escapes me
and it's as if I can no longer speak
I have to think of it
or else
to me
I'm a dead man

Je l'ai
sur le bout de la langue
Enfin c'est aux toilettes
qu'il me revient
Est-ce pour cette raison
qu'on parle de « lieux d'aisance » ?

I have it
on the tip of my tongue
Finally when I go to the bathroom
it comes back to me
Is that why
we call it "relieving" yourself?

Des tonnes de livres que j'ai lues
j'ai presque tout oublié
Suis-je devenu
un homme cultivé ?

Of the hundredweights of books I've read
I've forgotten almost everything
Have I become
a cultivated man?

Les athées
jurent leurs grands dieux
Les croyants
pestent contre les leurs

Atheists
swear by their special gods
Believers
curse their own

De cette feuille
dite vierge
que sortira-t-il
Un bouton de seringa
ou une fleur carnivore ?

C'est moi qui tremble

From this sheet of paper
we call virgin
what will come forth
A bud of mock-orange
or a carnivorous flower?

I'm the one trembling

Je n'ai pas entendu
la sentence
Et on me donne déjà
la dernière cigarette

I didn't hear
my sentence handed down
And already they're giving me
the last cigarette

Ils ont tout de l'homme
et ce ne sont pas des hommes
Regardez-les faire
ce qu'aucune bête
n'a jamais pu faire
Ils sont là
tapis en nous
qui nous prétendons hommes

They seem in every way like men
and they are not men
Look how they do
what no animal
has ever been able to do
They are there
crouched in us
we who claim to be human

N'importe quel enfant
vous le dira
l'histoire fait peur
et finit par endormir

Any kid
can tell you
history scares you
and ends up putting you to sleep

Depuis qu'il n'y a plus rien à dire
tout a été de nouveau dit
Et tourne manivelle !

Ever since there was nothing more to say
it's been said all over again
So give the crank another whirl!

Au lieu
d'égorger un mouton
pour la naissance d'un enfant
pourquoi ne pas planter un arbre ?

Instead
of slaughtering a sheep
at the birth of a child
why not plant a tree?

Par le plus pur des hasards
leurs regards se croisent
Ils se haïssent déjà

By the purest chance
their gazes met
Already they hate each other

Vernissage
Devant une toile
ils négocient
le prix d'une passe

A private opening
In front of a canvas
they negotiate
a hooker's price

Rire derrière moi
Rit-on de moi ?

Laughter behind me
Are they laughing *about* me?

Quand l'autre parle
je ne sais jamais
s'il faut que je fixe
ses yeux
ou ses lèvres

When someone is speaking
I never know
whether to stare
at his eyes
or his lips

Ne me convainc vraiment
que celui qui a
une dentition parfaite
ou à défaut
une lueur satanique
dans les pupilles

No one really convinces me
except the guy who has
perfect teeth
or failing that
pupils
with a satanic glint

Inassouvie
plus que rebelle
cette chair qui m'est tourment
Ma zone sismique
ma grande part animale
Il est temps
de se trahir
encore davantage

Insatiate
rather than rebellious
this flesh that is my torment
My seismic zone
my looming animal side
Now is the moment
to be betrayed
and this time even more

La naissance des seins
– comme c'est bien dit –
J'y regarde volontiers
oh jamais lourdement
Ai-je ou n'ai-je pas
une âme de voyeur ?

The first budding of breasts
—this expression is so lovely—
I always look
oh never really staring
Do I have—or not—
the soul of a voyeur?

On tombe amoureux
d'une passante
Puis vite
l'amour passe

You fall in love
with a passerby
Then quickly
love passes on

Serrer la main d'une femme
n'est jamais innocent

Shaking a woman's hand
is never innocent

Barcelone
La Rambla
Des centaines d'oiseaux soldés
s'égosillent dans leurs cages
conspuent les promeneurs
Les vendeurs
n'exigent plus
que le prix de leur silence

Barcelona
Las Ramblas
Hundreds of birds sold off
rending their throats in their cages
heckling the strolling crowd
The vendors now
ask only
the price of their silence

Bressuire
Place du Millénaire
la fontaine marocaine
érigée par des artisans de Fès
Qui aurait l'idée
de la reconduire à la frontière ?

Bressuire
Millenium Square
the Moroccan fountain
put up by artisans from Fez
Whose idea is it
to take it back to the Border?

Dimanche
Jardin du Luxembourg
On y manque d'air
tant la foule est compacte

Sunday
the Jardin du Luxembourg
You can't breathe
the crowd is so thick

De la vieille dame
ou de sa chienne
qui traîne l'autre ?
Image de la décrépitude
qui nous menace tous

Between the old lady
and her dog
who is dragging whom?
Image of decrepitude
threatening us all

Seul
au café
Les clients semblent s'étonner
de ma présence
La serveuse exige
d'être payée à l'avance
Je bois à coups rapides
pour me donner contenance
Le concert de l'indifférence
bat son plein
Je ne suis pas très fier
de moi

Alone
in the café
The drinkers seem amazed
at my presence
The waitress wants
to be paid in advance
I drink in quick gulps
to give myself composure
The concert of indifference
is in full swing
I'm not so proud
of myself

Attablé. Je me vois passer sur le trottoir d'en face. Une sacoche
à la main, l'habit un peu large, le dos légèrement voûté, la
tête franchement grise, le pas saccadé de quelqu'un qui sait
où il va, ou du moins veut donner cette impression, le regard
perçant des grands distraits, le vague sourire en coin de celui
à qui on ne la fait pas.

Tel que, le passant ne m'inspire ni sympathie ni antipathie. Je
ne fais rien pour lui signaler ma présence.

Je n'ai pas envie qu'on vienne troubler ma solitude.

At a table. I see myself go by on the opposite sidewalk. Sack
in hand, coat a bit too big, slightly stooped, a head—let's
face it—gone gray, the choppy steps of someone who knows
where he's going, or at least wants to give that impression,
the piercing gaze of the truly absent-minded, the vague, lop-
sided smile of someone who's nobody's fool.

With the result that this passerby inspires neither compassion
nor antipathy in me. I do nothing to make myself known to
him.

I don't want anyone coming to disturb my solitude.

IV

IV

« Chez moi », dit l'autre
avec naturel
Je me sens exclu
Il ne se doute de rien

"Home," says the other person
completely casual
I feel excluded
He doesn't suspect anything

La millième chambre d'hôtel
Les meubles me reconnaissent
Dehors
la ville m'ignore

The thousandth hotel room
The furnishings recognize me
Outside
the town doesn't know I'm here

Le mur d'en face
comme un miroir déformant
Les tuiles rouges
accentuent l'illusion
Je ne suis pas là
où je crois être

The wall across the way
like a fun-house mirror
The red roof tiles
sharpen the illusion
I am not
where I think I am

Une dame
à sa fenêtre
secoue énergiquement
un drap
Est-ce son compagnon
ou elle
qui fait tomber des miettes
en dormant ?

A lady
at her window
sharply shaking out
a sheet
Is her companion to blame
or does she
drop these crumbs
while asleep?

A ma droite
une ombre furtive
que j'efface d'un clignement de cils
Je refuse
de reconnaître les fantômes
surtout
quand ils manquent de courtoisie

Over to my right
a furtive shadow
that I erase with one quick blink
I refuse
to recognize ghosts
especially
when they lack simple courtesy

Tantôt le ciel me relie
Tantôt il me sépare
Toujours les nuages
me remettent à ma place

First the sky ties me together
Then it separates me
Always the clouds
settle me in my place again

Parallèles
le fleuve de l'oubli
le fleuve de la souvenance
Entre les deux
l'homme avance
pour mieux reculer
Ses pieds
restent secs

Parallels
the river of forgetting
the river of remembering
Between the two
man goes forth
all the better to retreat
His feet
stay dry

De ce pas
je ne vais nulle part

At this rate
I'm not going anywhere

Soudain
le futur
décomposé

Suddenly
the future
all decomposed

Vert et ocre
la terre démontée
Le tourbillon noir
des sachets en plastique
Le minaret
tombé du ciel
Puis la forêt
surgie des vagues
A reculons
la tempête

Green and ochre
earth collapsed
The black whirlwind
of plastic bags
The minaret
fallen from the sky
Then the forest
risen from the waves
And backing away
the storm

Le silence
et sa grâce
Prélude
à la voix intérieure

Silence
and its mercy
Prelude
to inner voice

Une rivière secrète
et sa source
tout aussi secrète
Si je pouvais m'y baigner
sans en troubler l'onde

A secret river
and its source
just as secret
If only I could swim there
and not disturb the ripples

Le toit du monde
J'y accède par à-coups
Je ne vois rien d'exceptionnel
La terre semble dormir
bercée par les vagues

The roof of the world
I reach it by fits and starts
I don't see anything special
The earth seems to sleep
gently rocked by waves

Le temps
que le Temps dévore
L'instant
une bouchée
dans ce banquet de la pénurie

Time
devoured by Time
The instant
a mouthful
in this banquet of dearth

Où suis-je ?
La question est risquée

Where am I?
The question has its risks

Je m'égare :
J'égare qui
et qui m'égare ?

I lead myself astray
Who am I leading
and who leads me?

La croyance me guette
Je fais mine
de ne pas m'en apercevoir

Faith stalks me
I act as if
unaware

Le soleil
dépose un rayon
sur le rebord de la fenêtre
Est-ce une allusion
Une invite ?
Qu'ai-je à lui offrir
en retour ?

The sun
leaves a ray
on the edge of the window
Is this an illusion
An invitation?
What can I offer
in return?

Souvenir lointain
Le bonheur m'a réveillé
Pour la première fois
j'avais connu l'amour
J'en vibrais encore
des pieds à la tête
J'avais quinze ans
et je me sentais immortel

A distant memory
Happiness awakened me
For the first time
I had known love
I was still tingling
head to toe
I was fifteen
and thought I was immortal

Un autre souvenir
Seul
entre quatre murs
Malgré la pénombre de rigueur
je pressens l'aube
L'esprit de l'aimée est là
plus ardent que sa chair
Ce poème muet
jamais je n'ai pu l'égaler

Another memory
Alone
among four walls
Despite the enforced gloom
I sense the dawn coming
The spirit of my beloved is there
more ardent than her flesh
That mute poem
I've never found its equal

Me réveiller auprès de toi
t'apporter le café
écouter ensemble la radio
accueillir ta tête sur mon épaule
te masser les doigts
L'amour simple
comme bonjour

Waking up next to you
bringing your coffee
listening to the radio together
cradling your head on my shoulder
massaging your fingers
love simple
as good morning

Tu es là
Tout n'est pas perdu

Devant toi
j'ai honte de mon désespoir

You are here
All is not lost

In front of you
I'm ashamed of my despair

V

V

La mouette

On ne remercie jamais assez les oiseaux
L'hôte d'aujourd'hui est une mouette
A son appel, je me suis mis à la fenêtre
A mon appel, elle s'est posée sur le toit
de la maison de Chateaubriand
Comme de vieilles connaissances
nous avons parlé de choses et d'autres
De la Méditerranée
venue jusqu'à Saint-Malo
Du ciel qui a revêtu enfin
sa cape bleue de cérémonie
Des vitraux de Bazaine
dans la maison vide de Dieu
Mais aussi de la solitude
qui s'empare de vous
au milieu de la foule
Merci, ai-je dit à la mouette
sans savoir pourquoi
Elle m'a répondu
par un petit ricanement complice
puis s'est envolée
vers Essaouira
ai-je pensé

The Seagull

We never thank birds quite enough
Today's guest is a seagull
At his call, I came to the window
At my call, it alighted on the roof
of Chateaubriand's house
Like old acquaintances
we chatted of one thing and another
Of the Mediterranean
come all the way to Saint-Malo
Of the sky throwing on at last
its ceremonial cloak of blue
Of the stained glass of Bazaine
in the empty house of God
But of that loneliness also
that comes over you
in the middle of a crowd
Thank you, I told the gull
without knowing why
It answered
with a snigger of complicity
then flew off
toward Essaouira
so it seemed

Chant de l'aube

(sur un tableau de Jean Bazaine)

De l'aube
je vois les chaînes
que tu écartes
d'un revers de lumière
comme si tu peignais
par compassion extrême
A peine as-tu trempé tes doigts
dans la source
l'océan du ciel frissonne sous la caresse
les couleurs ôtent leur suaire
pour s'adonner à l'étreinte
Ton chant que voilà
épris du blanc
que la mort daigne laisser
derrière elle
pour que nous autres vivants
y tracions nos marelles

Dawn Song

(on a painting by Jean Bazaine)

I see the chains
of this dawn
pulled aside by you
with a folding back of light
as if you were painting
with extreme sympathy
You have hardly dipped your fingers
in the source
the ocean of the sky shivers under that caress
the colors take off their shroud
and abandon themselves to embrace
Here is your song
smitten with the white
that death condescends
to leave behind
so we the living
can scratch our hopscotch with it

L'adieu au père

Le cheval hennit
au fond de la vieille ruelle
Son cri monte par les escaliers
pousse la porte de la terrasse
et fuse dans le ciel moutonneux
Les voix décalées des muezzins lui répondent
Les premiers beignets chauds embaument
et l'aube retient son souffle
Je suis là, ô mon alezan
malgré la distance
et le poids des ans
Je n'ai pas oublié de puiser l'eau pour toi
et de remplir ta mangeoire
Je t'écoute
Mon père referme la porte de la maison
Ses pas résonnent dans la vieille ruelle
et peu à peu s'éloignent

Adieu to Father

The horse neighs
deep in the old lane
Its cry winds up the stairways
pushes open the door to the terrace
and burns off in the fleecy sky
The staggered notes of the muezzins answer
The first warm fritters scent the air
and dawn holds its breath
I am here, oh my chestnut stallion
despite the distance
and the weight of years
I did not forget to draw your water
and fill your manger
I am listening to you
My father shuts the door of the house
His steps sound in the old lane
gain distance little by little

Je vous regardais d'en bas
maître du silence
et je ne reconnaissais d'autre trône
que votre échoppe d'artisan
Vous étiez juché
au milieu de cuirs et de cuivres
que vous rendiez
obéissants et rêveurs
Comment vos mains
auraient-elles pu se lever
pour frapper ?

Vous me disiez
« L'argent, ce n'est que la crasse du monde »
Vous aviez tout dit

I used to look on you from below
master of silence
and I knew no other throne
but your artisan's stall
You were perched
among the skins and copper
that you rendered
pensive and obedient
How could your hands ever
have risen
to strike?

You used to tell me
"Money is nothing but the world's filth"
You got that right

Le chat

Encore toi
les yeux fermés
ouverts sur le théâtre d'une autre vie
Cette maison immense
avec pour seule compagnie
le petit chat qui a flairé ta solitude
Il vient se frotter à toi
puis se love à tes pieds
Confiant
il rêve déjà
Voilà que tu te coules dans sa rêverie :
tu es un chat
L'homme seul qui gribouille à côté de toi
t'a caressé tout à l'heure
Il ne l'a pas fait distraitement
en pensant à sa femme
ou ses enfants
Et puisque la caresse t'était destinée
tu as ronronné d'aise
Maintenant
tu te sens en sécurité
Tu n'as pas faim
Tu n'as pas froid
Tu es comme dans le ventre de ta mère
Bientôt tu vas glisser
dans le doux tunnel qui conduit à la lumière
Mais comment sais-tu
qu'il y a une lumière au bout ?
Les yeux voient-ils avant que de s'ouvrir ?
Qui es-tu
petit chat
et d'où viens-tu ?

The Cat

Here you are again
eyes closed
yet opened on the theater of another life
This huge house
and no one for company but
the little cat that has sniffed out your solitude
It comes to rub against you
then curls at your feet
Trusting
and dreaming already
Now it is you who flow in its dreaming:
you are a cat
The solitary man scribbling beside you
caressed you just now
Nor did he do it absently
thinking of his wife
or his children
And since the caress was for you
you purred in comfort
Now
you feel secure
You're not hungry
You're not cold
You are as if in your mother's womb
Soon you will slip
through the gentle tunnel to the light
But how do you know
there is light at its end?
Do eyes see before they've been opened?
Who are you
little cat
and where do you come from?

La tourterelle

De ses cris
c'est un dieu de volupté
qu'elle invoque
Quel est le châtiment
de la tourterelle
quand elle blasphème ?

The Turtle Dove

With its cries
what it invokes
is a god of *volupté*
What punishment awaits
the turtle dove
when it blasphemes?

Incompréhension

Par grappes entières
les oiseaux ont occupé les arbres
et donnent leur concert
Ils savent que je les écoute
Je sais qu'ils veulent me dire quelque chose
De temps en temps
je crois saisir un mot
A son articulation
on dirait un vocable
de ma langue maternelle
prononcé avec l'accent du Sud
Je note à tout hasard :
Oui, non
reste, pars
la porte
dit-il
regarde
rien
derrière toi
Il a suffi que je prenne ces notes
pour que le concert s'arrête
Quel mot ai-je mal compris
pour faire taire ainsi les oiseaux ?

Not Understanding

In whole bunches
the birds have occupied the trees
and put on their concert
They know I'm listening
I know they want to tell me something
Now and again
I think I catch a word
From its pronunciation
it seems to be a phoneme
from my mother tongue
said in the southern accent
I pick out randomly:
Yes, no
stay, go
the door
he says
look
nothing
behind you
Just my taking these notes
has made the concert stop
What word did I get wrong
to quiet the birds this way?

Le monstre du train

C'est le même train
que je prends toujours
vers une vague destination
bondé
enfumé
avec le gosse criard de service
et la maman débordée
criant encore plus fort
Avec mon obèse de voisin
qui m'écrase et respire
sa portion d'air et la mienne
Avec mon bout de fenêtre
que je protège de la main
comme un écolier sa dictée
Avec la beauté fracassante
dont l'indifférence
fait déborder le vase

Le monstre tapi dans mon regard
va bientôt opérer
Ah j'en ai trucidé ainsi
des voyageurs
réduit en esclavage des reines
détruit des villes au passage
mis le feu à des frontières
et fait la nique à leurs cerbères
Pourtant
à ma connaissance
je ne fais l'objet
d'aucun avis de recherche

The Monster on the Train

It's the same train
I take every day
for a vague destination
jammed
smoky
with the shrill kid on duty
and the overflowing mom
yelling even louder
With my obese neighbor
who squishes me and breathes
his portion of the air and mine
With my corner of window
that I protect with my hand
the way a student covers his classwork
With that shattering beauty
whose indifference
puts me over the top

The monster crouching in my gaze
will soon spring into action
Ah, I have bumped off
travelers
reduced queens to slavery
destroyed villages in my path
set frontiers ablaze
and nodded in passing to each Cerberus
Still
as far as I'm aware
I'm not the object
of any arrest warrant

Les îles éternelles

à A. Alvarez de la Rosa

Sindbad a fait le tour du monde
en six jours
Et le septième
voulant se reposer
il accosta dans ces îles
Il les trouva presque désertes
et se dit : Cela est bien !
Ici la terre prend tout son temps
pour naître
Elle veut écouter jusqu'à la fin
les mille et une histoires de l'Océan
Elle sème dans le miroir du ciel
ses premiers rêves de langues, d'arbres
et de visages humains
Elle caresse son ventre et ses seins volcaniques
pour que le feu pactise avec l'eau
et nous apprête la page d'amour
qui manque au livre de la vie
O îles, s'écria Sindbad
promettez-moi une genèse douce
un autre art de naître
Ecoutez
Semez
Caressez
Rêvez pour toute la terre
et vous mériterez le nom que je vous donne :
Îles éternelles

The Eternal Isles

for A. Alvarez de la Rosa

Sinbad went round the world
in six days
And on the seventh
wishing to take his rest
he drew up in these islands
He found them almost deserted
and said to himself: It is good!
Here the land takes her time
being born
She wants to hear to the end
the thousand and one tales of the Ocean
She sows in the mirror of the sky
her first dreams of languages, trees
and human faces
She caresses her belly and volcanic breasts
to make fire come to terms with water
and prepare for us that page on love
missing from the book of life
Oh isles, cried Sinbad
promise me a sweet genesis
a different art of being born
Listen
Sow
Caress
Dream for all the earth
and you will deserve my name for you:
Eternal Isles

Réalité

Me voici de nouveau dans ma banlieue
Cette maison
que je changerai encore pour une autre
La pièce où je ne m'enferme plus pour écrire
(je ne suis pas à une contradiction près)
Ce que m'offre ma fenêtre
un bout de rue
où passent plus de voitures que de piétons
Un pan de ciel opaque
si bas
que les oiseaux s'y cognent les ailes
Sur mon bureau
les lettres se sont entassées
Sous mon coude
des poèmes inachevés
A côté
la machine à laver tourne
fait disparaître de mes habits
l'odeur du voyage
Voici que le téléphone sonne
Tel un automate
je tends la main
et me rends à la réalité

Reality

Here I am again in my neighborhood
This house
that I'll change yet again for another
The room where I no longer shut myself in to write
(well, with one exception)
What my window offers me
a stretch of road
where more cars go by than pedestrians
A patch of sky opaque
and so low
that the birds bump wings
On my desk
the letters have piled up
Under my elbow
unfinished poems
At my side
the washing machine revolves
makes the smell of travel
vanish from my clothes
Now the telephone rings
Like an automaton
I stretch forth my hand
and surrender to reality

DIÁLOGOS
BOOKS
dialogosbooks.com